U0027614

Little People, **BIG DREAMS**
ROSA PARKS

Little People, **BIG DREAMS**

ROSA PARKS

Written by
Lisbeth Kaiser

Illustrated by
Marta Antelo

Frances Lincoln
Children's Books

Rosa grew up near Montgomery, Alabama, with her mother, brother and grandparents.

She was very little and very brave, and she always tried to do what was right.

When she was young, Rosa's grandparents told her stories about slavery, when black people weren't free to live like other people.

Slavery was over, but times were still hard for Rosa and her family. Black people were treated very badly and told they were not equal to white people.

Every day, Rosa watched the school bus go by taking white children to their big school. It didn't stop for her. She had to walk a long way to the one-room school that was just for black children.

Rosa knew this wasn't right. She knew she was a regular person, just as good as anyone else.

Lots of times, she had to make sure other people knew it too.

When Rosa grew up and got a job in the city, she couldn't use the same doors, lifts, bathrooms or water fountains as white people.

COLOURED

WHITE

COLOURED
WAITING ROOM

COLOURED
ENTRANCE

She could ride the bus, but she had to sit at the back. Her life was full of rules that she knew weren't right.

Rosa fell in love with a man named Raymond who was trying to change the rules to be more fair and equal.

Soon Rosa started working, too, trying to get more rights for black people and help for those who were treated badly. She worked day after day, even when it seemed like nothing would ever change.

On her way home from the city one day, a bus driver
told Rosa to stand up so a white person could take her
seat. She was sick of rules that she knew were wrong.
She thought, *enough*. She said, "No".

Rosa was taken to jail. She wasn't scared, because she knew that what she was fighting for was right.

When Rosa came home that night, she talked with her friends and family about what to do. She decided to keep fighting, no matter how hard it would be.

Black people all over the city heard what had happened to Rosa.
They thought, *enough*.

Rosa inspired them to stop riding the buses until the rules changed.

So they walked, to school and to work and to the shops, in all kinds of weather.

Rosa travelled the country – from New York to San Francisco – to convince other people to join the fight.

ALABAMA JOURNAL

LATEST EDITION

BUS SEGREGATION IS KNOCKED OUT

Finally, after one year, the Supreme Court decided that treating black people differently from white people on buses was wrong. The rules were going to change!

It was no longer safe for Rosa to live in Alabama. She moved to Detroit and fought for fair schools, jobs and houses for black people.

She fought for voting rights, women's rights
and the rights of people in prison.

When Rosa was an older woman, she was given awards and told she was a hero. But she knew who she was.

A regular person, just as good as anyone else. And she had work to do.

ROSA PARKS

(Born 1913 • Died 2005)

c. 1950

1955

Rosa Parks was an American activist and one of the most important figures in the civil rights movement. The grandchild of former slaves, she grew up with her mother, brother and grandparents on a small farm outside of Montgomery, Alabama, where she faced mean and unfair treatment because of her skin colour. She regularly resisted with bravery and dignity. It wasn't until she met her husband, Raymond Parks, that she learned about activism. At 30, she became a leader in the National Association for the Advancement of Coloured People (NAACP) in Montgomery and began working to end inequality.

1965   1984

When she was 42, Rosa was taken from a bus and jailed because
she refused to give her seat to a white person. Her arrest brought
the black people of Montgomery together to demand change and
she helped lead them in a year-long boycott of the buses. Rosa's
actions and hard work helped establish the civil rights movement.
They also cost her family their jobs and safety. They moved north
to Detroit, where Rosa was dismayed to find that great inequality
persisted. She remained an activist for the rest of her life, helping
many people and inspiring countless others with her bravery, dignity
and determination in the ongoing fight for human equality.

Want to find out more about **Rosa Parks**?

She has written a book about her life:

I am Rosa Parks by Rosa Parks and James Haskins

You could also try these:

I am Rosa Parks by Brad Meltzer

Who Was Rosa Parks? by Yona Zeldis McDonough

And if you're near the Henry Ford Museum in Michigan, you could even visit the famous Rosa Parks bus.

Brimming with creative inspiration, how-to projects, and useful information to enrich your everyday life, Quarto Knows is a favourite destination for those pursuing their interests and passions. Visit our site and dig deeper with our books into your area of interest: Quarto Creates, Quarto Cooks, Quarto Homes, Quarto Lives, Quarto Drives, Quarto Explores, Quarto Gifts, or Quarto Kids.

First published in the UK in 2017 by Frances Lincoln Children's Books,
an imprint of The Quarto Group, The Old Brewery, 6 Blundell Street, London N7 9BH
www.QuartoKnows.com

Text copyright © 2017 by Lisbeth Kaiser. Illustrations copyright © 2017 by Marta Antelo.

This book has not been authorised or endorsed by the Rosa Parks Estate. Any mistakes herein are the fault of the publishers, who would be happy to rectify them on a future printing.

Commissioned as part of the Little People, Big Dreams series,
conceived by Mª Isabel Sánchez Vegara.
Originally published under the title Pequeña & Grande by Alba Editorial (www.albaeditorial.es)

All rights reserved

Translation rights arranged by IMC Agència Literària, SL

No part of this publication may be reproduced, stored in a retrieval system, or transmitted,
in any form, or by any means, electrical, mechanical, photocopying, recording or otherwise without the prior written permission of the publisher or a licence permitting restricted copying. In the United Kingdom such licences are issued by the Copyright Licensing Agency, Barnard's Inn, 86 Fetter Lane, London, EC4A 1EN.

A catalogue record for this book is available from the British Library.

ISBN 978-1-78603-017-7

Published by Rachel Williams • Designed by Karissa Santos
Edited by Katy Flint • Production by Kate O'Riordan
Manufactured in Guangdong, China CC082020

13

Photographic acknowledgements (pages 28-29, from left to right) 1. Rosa Parks Collection at the Library of Congress, 2015 © The Washington Post, Getty Images 2. Rosa Louise McCauley Parks booking photo, 1955 © Universal Images Group, Getty Images 3. Selma to Montgomery March, 1965 © Stephen F. Somerstein, Getty Images 4. Rosa Parks protesting apartheid, 1984 © Bettman, Getty Images

Collect the
Little People, BIG DREAMS series:

FRIDA KAHLO

ISBN: 978-1-84780-770-0

COCO CHANEL

ISBN: 978-1-84780-771-7

MAYA ANGELOU

ISBN: 978-1-84780-890-5

AMELIA EARHART

ISBN: 978-1-84780-885-1

AGATHA CHRISTIE

ISBN: 978-1-84780-959-9

MARIE CURIE

ISBN: 978-1-84780-961-2

ROSA PARKS

ISBN: 978-1-78603-017-7

AUDREY HEPBURN

ISBN: 978-1-78603-052-8

EMMELINE PANKHURST

ISBN: 978-1-78603-019-1

ELLA FITZGERALD

ISBN: 978-1-78603-086-3

ADA LOVELACE

ISBN: 978-1-78603-075-7

JANE AUSTEN

ISBN: 978-1-78603-119-8

GEORGIA O'KEEFFE

ISBN: 978-1-78603-121-1

HARRIET TUBMAN

ISBN: 978-1-78603-289-8

ANNE FRANK

ISBN: 978-1-78603-292-8

MOTHER TERESA

ISBN: 978-1-78603-290-4

JOSEPHINE BAKER

ISBN: 978-1-78603-291-1

L. M. MONTGOMERY

ISBN: 978-1-78603-295-9

JANE GOODALL

ISBN: 978-1-78603-294-2

SIMONE DE BEAUVOIR

ISBN: 978-1-78603-293-5

MUHAMMAD ALI

ISBN: 978-1-78603-733-6

STEPHEN HAWKING

ISBN: 978-1-78603-732-9

MARIA MONTESSORI

ISBN: 978-1-78603-753-4

VIVIENNE WESTWOOD

ISBN: 978-1-78603-756-5

MAHATMA GANDHI

ISBN: 978-1-78603-334-5

DAVID BOWIE

ISBN: 978-1-78603-803-6

WILMA RUDOLPH

ISBN: 978-1-78603-750-3

DOLLY PARTON

ISBN: 978-1-78603-759-6

BRUCE LEE

ISBN: 978-1-78603-335-2

RUDOLF NUREYEV

ISBN: 978-1-78603-336-9

ZAHA HADID

ISBN: 978-1-78603-744-2

MARY SHELLEY

ISBN: 978-1-78603-747-3

MARTIN LUTHER KING JR.

ISBN: 978-0-7112-4566-2

DAVID ATTENBOROUGH

ISBN: 978-0-7112-4563-1

ASTRID LINDGREN

ISBN: 978-1-78603-762-6

EVONNE GOOLAGONG

ISBN: 978-0-7112-4585-3

BOB DYLAN

ISBN: 978-0-7112-4674-4

ALAN TURING

ISBN: 978-0-7112-4677-5

BILLIE JEAN KING

ISBN: 978-0-7112-4692-8

GRETA THUNBERG

ISBN: 978-0-7112-5643-9

JESSE OWENS

ISBN: 978-0-7112-4582-2

JEAN-MICHEL BASQUIAT

ISBN: 978-0-7112-4579-2

ARETHA FRANKLIN

ISBN: 978-0-7112-4687-4

CORAZON AQUINO

ISBN: 978-0-7112-4683-6

PELÉ

ISBN: 978-0-7112-4574-7

ERNEST SHACKLETON

ISBN: 978-0-7112-4570-9

STEVE JOBS

ISBN: 978-0-7112-4576-1

AYRTON SENNA

ISBN: 978-0-7112-4671-3

LOUISE BOURGEOIS

ISBN: 978-0-7112-4689-8

ELTON JOHN

ISBN: 978-0-7112-5838-9